George Dolnikowski

George Dolnikowski

Christopher Raschka

ILLUSTRATOR

*faith*Quest

BRETHREN PRESS

This I Remember

D1376761

from War to Peace

Copyright © 1994 by *faithQuest*. Published by Brethren Press, 1451 Dundee Avenue, Elgin, Illinois 60120

Designed by Randy Maid

98   97   96   95   94   5   4   3   2   1

Library of Congress Cataloging-in-Publication Data

Dolnikowski, George, 1918-
   This I remember : from war to peace / George Dolnikowski;
Christopher Raschka, illustrator.
     p.   cm.
   ISBN 0-87178-849-7
   1. Dolnikowski, George, 1918- . 2. Russian Americans—Biography. I. Title.
E184.R9D653   1994
973'.049171—dc20

94-12609

Manufactured in the United States of America

Dedication

I wish to dedicate my book to Dr. Calvert N. Ellis, former president of Juniata College. In 1948 he was moderator of the Annual Conference of the Church of the Brethren when the Brethren Volunteer Service (BVS) program was born, a forerunner of President John F. Kennedy's Peace Corps. BVS was incorporated into the ongoing work of the Brethren Service Commission, which included the refugee resettlement program through which I came to the United States in 1949. Dr. Ellis brought me to Juniata College. I first worked there as a janitor. On his invitation four years later, I joined the faculty.

Contents

Foreword

*T*hese pages document the unusual encounter after 1949 of a Russian intellectual—buffeted by personal tragedies following the Bolshevik Revolution and painful existence for years as a prisoner-of-war in Nazi Germany—with faculty and students on the campus of Juniata College in Central Pennsylvania. George Dolnikowski was one of thousands of "displaced persons" resettled in the United States after World War II by the Brethren Service Commission, the social action arm of the Church of the Brethren. Juniata College is the oldest college (1876) affiliated with the Church of the Brethren.

The Brethren movement began in early eighteenth-century Germany among a small group of refugees who had been driven from their homes by religious persecution. Most came from the Palatinate, the scene of bloody conflict during the Thirty Years War (1618-1648) and repeated invasions by French armies at the end of the century. Those who became Brethren had bitter experience of war and homelessness. It is not surprising that they became passionately dedicated to peacemaking and reaching out to help those in need. Early records indicate that their life together was marked by concern for the bodily and spiritual care of their fellows.

In reaction to an arbitrary and harsh ecclesiastical establishment that demanded doctrinal submission while permitting laxness and worse in personal conduct among members and leaders, the Brethren placed more emphasis on living their faith than correctly defining it. They refused to set down a written creed that had to be adhered to by all believers, preferring to claim the whole New Testament as their guideline for faith and practice. They called for life service rather than lip service.

This orientation helps to explain the impressive record since 1708 of mutual aid among their own ranks and sacrificial service to those outside their membership who suffered because of natural disaster, social conflicts, or the agonies of war. Unprecedented worldwide deprivation brought about by World War II and its aftermath was ameliorated in a number of creative ways by Brethren, who often initiated programs of relief and rehabilitation later adopted by other religious bodies. Among these were the Heifer Project, the CROP organization for material aid, the high school student exchange program (ICYE), the New Windsor (Maryland) Service Center, and others. Brethren were also among the creators of the ecumenical Church World Service plan, still meeting need around the world in the 1990s.

Those Brethren who gave years of their lives in uncompensated labor for these and similar programs are quick to testify that they gained personally from these involvements. They speak of these volunteer years as broadening their horizons, enriching their cultural awareness, and, most importantly, as enabling new friendships across national boundaries.

Some of those new friendships made possible by Brethren service activity are documented in these memoirs by George Dolnikowski. He was placed on the campus of Juniata College through the refugee resettlement program of the Brethren Service Commission; along with thousands of others, he was helped to make a new start and find a new home in the United States. Fortunately there were sensitive souls at Juniata who recognized, beyond the linguistic barrier, the intellectual depths and personal qualities of the newcomer; they helped to make it possible for the janitor to prepare for and become a college professor.

These memoirs demonstrate in moving ways not only how a few unselfish actions profited one individual, but also how his new life has enriched generations of students. George Dolnikowski's passion for peace and human goodwill—won despite much harsh personal tragedy—has proved fruitful in many different ways. Vignettes and anecdotes, described in simple but eloquent words, illustrate one man's quest for personal and international peace. Truly the biblical image of "bread cast upon the waters" has come true in this life, as the aid extended to the author by Brethren has been repaid manyfold by his life and witness.

—*Donald F. Durnbaugh*

Acknowledgments

Sincere thanks to Lucy Heggenstaller and Kathleen Achor-Hoch for inspiring me to write this story, to Joanne Dolnikowski and Peter Sandler for reading and editing the text, to Verna Horne and Evelyn Pembrooke for typing the manuscript, and to Klare Sunderland for helping to finance the book's publication.

Childhood

I remember my parents through whom I am related to everyone, whether living or dead.

I remember two teenage sisters, daughters of our neighbor, who took care of me when my mother was sick and wounded and my father was away fighting in the civil war. These sisters saved my life. The country was torn apart by the war and underwent famine and a typhus epidemic.

I remember the tic-toc tic-toc sound of my mother's crutches on the hardwood floor.

I remember playing in the sandbox with the children of a German teacher. They infected me with the German language.

I remember my first day of school. It began with a vaccination and tears.

I remember a most treasured toy, a large cardboard box. It became the world to me. A house, a school, a boat, whatever I desired it to be.

I remember my childhood, filled with visions of ghosts, sprites, and witches in every conceivable dark place: in the attic, on the bottom of the river, in the woods, in the well... My parents always told me not to be late when I played in the evening, because the ghosts could burn a person by just flying overhead, especially after midnight.

I remember the unearthly fragrance of my uncle's sunflower processing plant. It produced oils and candies. I remember the candy best, succulent and caramel sweet.

I remember the church services my father took me to after he returned from fighting. The Russian Orthodox service was hours long, but beautiful and mystic. One was caught up in the ebb and flow of standing and kneeling, the flickering light of a hundred candles, the fragrance of frankincense, the resonance of deep choral singing, chants, the icons, the kissing of the cross…

I remember prayer. My father and I knelt every morning in the holy corner of our *izba* (cottage) while my mother rekindled the fire. Before and after each meal, we prayed, and before I could let myself fall asleep, I prayed; for one does not know what might happen in the night, and as a child "what might" is particularly vivid.

I remember the experiences of eating the first apple, the first tomato, the first cucumber in early summer. So tasty, so fragrant. In Russia, if you really love your girl, you call her "my dear sweet little cucumber." One does not appreciate all this freshness if it is available all year round.

I remember a teaglassful of vodka I drank at my brother's wedding. He wanted to show how tough I was for my nine years. It laid me out for two days and nights, with my mother watching over me all this time while I was lying under an apple tree in our orchard.

I remember summer nights with my friend on a haystack. Before we'd fall asleep we'd talk about our favorite girls. How can one forget the first walk with a girl, the first embrace?

I remember the good times before collectivization took place in Russia. On Sunday afternoon the whole neighborhood would play a game with one base and an unlimited number of players on each team. The best part of the game was that, win or lose, everybody had a marvelous time.

I remember the Easter holidays after a long, cold winter. Suddenly it was springtime, complete with new life, new hope—in a word, resurrection. There was a week of festivities: games, good food, and fellowship. Above all, there were the church services and the blessing of all life by the priest.

I remember the traveling circus: actors, animal trainers, jugglers, magicians, muscle men ...

I remember one man who played the Russian accordion for those who wanted to dance. He played folk tunes so well that I was jealous of his ability. I wanted to play the instrument so that I could express myself—especially to tell my girl how much I loved her.

I remember my first fight with a boy who called me Saint Francis. In Russia at that time, anything related to religion was considered obscene. I hit him hard on the nose. He streaked my face with scratches.

I remember my grandmother making cherry jelly. I helped her by licking the pots and spoons.

I remember a dream. At home we had a park, and in that park there was a small pond. I dreamed I was coming to that pond to see my reflection. Suddenly the bank gave in, and I fell into the water. I tried to get out, but each time I would climb and then slip farther back, until finally the whole bank fell in. I began shouting.

Then I felt the hand of my mother. I awoke and she asked, "What is it?" I told her about my bad dream.

A few days later she went to a fortune-teller, a gypsy, and told her about the dream. The fortune-teller told her, "Someday your son will go away and will never return."

I remember a slogan that hung firmly over the blackboard in our elementary school: *dognat' i peregnat' amerikanskuyu kuritsu.* Catch up with and surpass the American Chicken.

I remember going to the river with my father to collect reeds, the only means we had to heat our house. After my father was arrested, I had to do it by myself. My mind can see the wolf tracks in the snow even more clearly now than then.

I remember a tiny bouquet of snowdrops I picked for Eugenia. I planned to hand them to her and run away before she could respond. But I couldn't come up with the courage to do it.

I remember two of my cousins whose father was a cavalry man. They made fun of me, saying, "He can't climb a horse on his own. He needs someone to help him." I wanted to tell them that I had better grades in school than they had. I kept quiet, but inside I had all sorts of things to say.

I remember when I was in third grade teaching an official of the collective farm how to read and write. He paid me with half a loaf of bread for one lesson. I was eleven years old at that time. I remember that his wife was very beautiful. She knew that I had eyes for her. I was jealous that she was his and not mine, although I really did not know at that time what it was to belong to someone.

I remember a picture I drew of Stalin on the blackboard before I went out for recess. Someone else sketched in a man with a pistol pointed at Stalin. I was thrown out of school. My father had to go and explain to the school authorities about my "ideological upbringing."

I remember my first swimming lesson. The water sprite terrified me!

I remember secretly smoking my first cigarette. Its scent still lingers, though I don't smoke at all.

I remember being left alone in a field about ten miles from home. I wanted to stay there by myself to prove that I was brave. I had to prepare a meal all on my own. While I was chopping wood, I hurt myself. After fifty-five years, I still have a scar to remind me of that day. But I had my meal that night: a soup made of potatoes and millet.

I remember when my friend Peter and I decided to go into our neighbor's cherry orchard. It was a beautiful orchard, full of dark, sweet cherries. We thought we would go on Sunday, believing our neighbor would be in church.

We climbed over the fence and each of us chose a cherry tree to climb. We started picking the cherries, eating some of them while putting the others into bags. Suddenly Peter shouted, "Nikita is coming!"

I was frightened, so instead of climbing down, I jumped. I fell on my bag of cherries, smashing them. Because it was Sunday, I was wearing a new shirt—one that my mother had worked very hard to find the material for. But I couldn't worry about that yet. Nikita was in sight. We jumped over the fence, ran through the back fields, crossed the river, and hid in the woods.

Finally we decided we had reached safety. But then I saw my shirt—it looked like a modern painting! I was almost crying.

Peter said, "Don't worry, we'll go down to the river and wash it." So we went back to the river, and I took off my shirt and began washing it. The spots were still there so I decided to scrub it with a little sand. I rubbed and rubbed until I realized there was a little hole. It was then that I realized I would have to answer to my mother.

By then it was noon. Peter suggested, "Why don't we wait here until it gets dark? Then we'll go home and you'll go to bed and everything will be all right."

We waited and waited. The time passed so slowly. When it was finally dark, we went home.

The door was locked when I got there. I decided to climb through the window. Just as I was stepping onto the bench inside, I heard my mother's voice in the dark, "Where were you?"

I was frightened and started crying. I said, "Mother, forgive me. My friend Peter and I decided to go stealing cherries."

"I know everything," my mother told me. "Nikita was here complaining. The only thing for you to do now is to go to bed without supper. I hope you will remember this day as long as you live." I have. "Tomorrow you have to talk to your father."

My father had been very angry with me at times, but he had never spanked me. However, I thought that the next morning could be the day. I fell asleep thinking of all the things that could happen.

I awoke to a bright, sunny morning. I went to my father immediately. He was ready to go to work in our orchard. He asked me, "What should I do with you?"
I replied, "Do anything, but please forgive me."

He looked at me and said, "I talked with your mother and we decided that this is the last time you will do this unpunished."

I promised not to steal cherries any more at any place, and I never did.

I remember my grandmother who pilgrimaged by foot for three months to Jerusalem. She returned with a tiny vial of tears of Saint Mary and fingernails of Jesus. She believed. I didn't.

I remember fairy tales my grandmother used to tell me, especially one that was about a boy who came to know what fear was. I came to know what fear was too, but not from fairy tales.

I remember the singing of the local choir made up of the peasant women at home. The doleful songs came from their hearts, expressing melancholy and yearning for better times. My mother was among them.

I remember being among those boys whose duty it was to stay out all night to keep watch over the horses in the meadow field. The older ones recounted tales of witches and spirits and told about their love affairs.

I remember taking part in a play and dreaming of becoming an actor.

I remember the burning of our church. I can still picture the belfry bells tumbling down from the flaming tower. It was said that the Communists torched it.

I remember when my father was jailed and all things of worth were confiscated from our house. My favorite possession, my boots—thick leathered as a man's—were taken by the local Communists.

I remember going through the fields of the co-op farm gleaning single heads of grain. At home my mother and I would clean and hull it, rubbing it between our hands.

I remember digging in the frozen ground for leftover potatoes, turnips, and sugar beets, the top inch of mud and debris sticking for a long time to my shoes, with the earth underneath hard as a stone.

I remember the famine in the late 1930s. One day, in exchange for weaving a tablecloth, my mother received two potatoes. We decided we would each eat one. Then I went to the river, hoping I could catch some fish. I caught several and divided my catch in two. I looked around and found some wild onions. One potato, wild onions, and fish—I had a meal I'll never forget. Hunger is the best cook.

I remember running through pine woods with an open pail of milk. Lightning flashed, casting devils' shadows; thunder pounded inside my head; there were spirits and witches around just out of sight. Finally I made it home, wet with tears, rain, and most of the milk.

I remember sneaking away by night from the state farm where I worked in season, the darkness concealing weeks' worth of saved bread and some kerosene for my mother. I remember the ensuing twelve miles of aching feet and jittery nerves, and I still see the spirits of my childhood in the shadows.

I remember visiting my father in the local prison. He was put there because he refused to join a local collective farm and because he would not renounce his orthodox faith. He sat on the floor killing louse after louse. Dozens of men shared that cell and those lice.

Away from Home

I remember a time when I was an assistant in the Institute of Foreign Languages. One of my duties was to show films. In order to operate the projector, I had to crank it with my hand. In this way I could control the speed of the projection. When there was a horse race or a boxing match, I would crank as fast as I could. When there was a kissing scene, I would go very slowly. However, I could not be too slow because the film would burn.

I remember working in the lab. I built a shortwave radio to pierce the Iron Curtain from inside out.

I remember that when my year was over at the Institute I decided to go home to visit my parents. As soon as I arrived, I sensed that changes had occurred. The house looked deserted. I entered from the back.

When I opened the door to the living room I found it full of pigs. I looked into the kitchen area. There, in the middle of the room, was a furnace with a huge kettle. In the kettle was an enormous horse leg, boiling in the water. Steam filled the room, which along with the fire made me feel as though I'd just entered a kitchen of hell.

Naturally, my first concern was for my parents. I left the house. A neighbor recognized me and greeted me. I returned her greeting and asked her what had happened. My parents had been exiled to Siberia, she told me, and if I wanted to avoid the same fate I should go away as fast as I could.

I did not waste time. It was twilight, and I headed for the railroad station. I boarded a train at 2:00 A.M. I never saw my house or my native village again.

I now recall that in that hellish room the icons of my childhood were still in the holy corner. At that moment they didn't have much meaning for me as I was overwhelmed with the tremendous changes that had hit me. The icons had held so much meaning for me as a child. They hold more meaning for me now than at the time of that visit.

I remember that, as a student at the Institute, I often received tickets to the symphony or theater or circus. One time I had two tickets to the circus. I invited a girl to go with me and she accepted! I was very happy. I told her (since she lived close) to meet me there. I would come by streetcar, for only a few officials had cars of their own.

It was Saturday. I had cleaned and pressed my suit, my hair was combed, and I was ready for my date. I had to walk several blocks to get to the streetcar. I got on and was heading toward the circus, when suddenly I realized I'd forgotten my tickets. I got off at the next stop, got on a car to go back home, picked up the tickets—they were right there on the desk—and got back on the streetcar heading toward my destination.

There was no stop right by the circus. The closest one was almost two blocks past it. But because the streetcar was turning and moving slowly, I decided to jump. And just as I did, I ran into a policeman.

"Don't you know this is illegal?" the policeman asked me.

"I know," I said. "But look—I'm late, there is a girl waiting for me whom I'm meeting for the first time. See, I have the tickets."

"Let me see your identification," he said.

I didn't have it with me. And in Russia, God help the man without identification. I had to go to the police station. I was almost in tears, swearing that I would come back, showing him the tickets. But they had to call still another high official concerning what to do.

By the time it was over, an hour had passed, and it was still a distance from the station to the circus. But when I got there, she was still waiting!

She looked at me and said, "I didn't know what to do. Either you had completely forgotten or something had happened."

I assured her that something had happened. We became very good friends. We had good times together, but the war separated us. While working in a hospital, she was killed by a bomb from a German plane during the early months of the war.

I remember when the head of my Institute recommended me as an instructor to the leader of the Communist Party in our district.

I remember the house with two telephones at a time when most institutions had only one. One phone was red, a direct line to Moscow. The other, a black one, was for the personal use of my host, the district party head. The power of those telephones, the power of the system, made a profound impression on me.

I remember waiting for a train in Moscow to go to Leningrad. It was night, and I fell asleep in the chair, leaning over the back. When I awoke, I couldn't move. I was petrified—I thought I was paralyzed! But after several minutes my ability to move began to return. First I could raise my head, and eventually I could move my whole body.

The train to Leningrad was so full of people that one could hardly move about, even on the third level. It was summertime and very hot, but who cared? I was on my way to Leningrad. It was my reward for good study.

But on the way back to Moscow, we were placed on an international train for diplomats. What a difference in accommodations! Even different colors of lights had a purpose—the blue one to calm you, so I was told.

I remember being on the White Sea-Baltic Sea Canal, built completely of wood by forced labor. It is said that Stalin built it, but everyone knows many thousands died there constructing it. We were told always to be on the lookout for foreign spies and, in this case, to watch for spies who would try to discover the secrets of the canal construction.

I remember that four things especially impressed me while in Leningrad: Alexander Nevsky's sarcophagus; the chess gallery in the Hermitage; the spot where Alexander Pushkin, Russia's greatest poet, stood during the duel in which he was mortally wounded; and the opportunity to see a piece of Finland from the observation platform at St. Isaac's.

I remember the frustrations of a part-time job in an airplane factory: translating German technical literature into Russian without access to a dictionary.

I remember becoming a bona fide instructor of German before the war when German was popular in Russian schools.

I remember that when I was a student we played war games on the meadow. Two opposing forces would fight. There would be units with fake guns and ammunition.

How primitive it all seems when only a few years later there was a real war. How positive we were about the strength of the Soviet Union. How much we had talked about preparedness and about how well we were prepared. But when Hitler came, all this was smashed to pieces. Russia lost over twenty million people. So many governmental declarations were buried by the war. But the memory remains.

Army and Imprisonment

I remember Molotov's announcement, Sunday, the twenty-second of July, 1941, at 12:00 noon, as I ate borsch and black bread: Germany had attacked Russia. The Russians had waited eight hours to receive the horrible news.

I remember the political commissar in the division of the Red Army who asked me, "Why do you speak German? Do you have relatives in Germany?"

"No," I told him, "I'm a teacher."

"We'll see," he said.

I remember being armed with only a pistol when I took part in an attack against German tanks.

I remember seeing during the battle a wounded soldier whose chest was open so that I could see his lungs expanding and contracting. He shouted, "Please help me." I continued running …

I remember being wounded on the third of October, 1941. I was captured the same day. I remember the first morning in captivity. The night before, I had a beautiful dream, and then how different was the reality when I awoke. I saw many German soldiers. Inscribed on their belt buckles was *"Gott mit uns"* (God with us). For the first time, I seriously questioned, Who is God?

When I became a prisoner, the German interrogators asked, "Why do you speak such fluent German? Are you a Communist?"

"No," I said, "I'm a teacher."

The commander of the division himself wanted to find out whether I was a teacher or not. He gave an order to find a teacher among the German soldiers. They brought the teacher, and the commander said to him, "Talk to this fellow about your profession."

After our conversation about teaching foreign languages, about difficulties in teaching German—I told him about the subjunctive, passive, and indirect speech—the German teacher said to the commander, "I can sign to testify that he is a teacher."

The commander replied, "You are a stupid ass. He is a perfect spy." Then he said to me, "That's all right. You'll stay with us and work. We'll see." It was exactly the same thing the Russian commissar had said to me.

I remember a mechanical pencil given to me by the German soldier who helped to identify me as a German teacher while I was in prison. Days later he came to me and said, "I'm going to the front line to fight the Russians. I don't want to go, but I am ordered. It is my duty and my fate. I don't know what will happen to me, but here is something I would like you to remember me by." Now, after so many years, I still have this sterling silver pencil, which I have polished many times since the war. This is the best souvenir I have from the war, and I will treasure it all my life.

After several weeks I had recovered enough to be able to walk. My left arm had healed as well. I was with the *Gefangenensammelstelle*, a unit that took care of the prisoners for the first few days or weeks. The sergeant of this unit watched me and talked to me quite a bit during my stay. He was a very serious man. It is quite possible that someone had suggested that I was a Russian spy.

It was fall. In Russia, the fall is very wet. There is mud everywhere, and there are no roads to speak of. One evening the sergeant said, "Come with me." We went to a school where the unit was quartered. He took off his boots, took a shoe shine kit from his bag, threw the boots at me, and said, "Shine them. Don't use a knife—here's a wooden plate. Don't scratch them." He left.

There was a German soldier in the room who told me, "You had better clean them well. One Russian prisoner tried to tell him he was an officer. He was executed on the grounds that he wanted to escape. I advise you to follow his commands."

I told the soldier that I had an officer's rank, although I was not in active service. I was an interpreter without any experience in the army. Still I felt it was against the rules.

"Rules?" he laughed. "What do you mean, rules?"

I wondered what I should do. Should I put my principles above my life? I thought to myself, I want to live as long as I can. I cannot fulfill the dream of the Red Army: to fight for the glory of Russia, for the glory of Communism. I am in prison. Under these circumstances, my dream is to save my life.

I shined the boots.

The sergeant returned, inspected his boots, and said, "Not bad." Then he ordered me to go with a soldier to make sure the prisoners were locked up for the night. (When prisoners came, it was my job to translate the orders that they all surrender anything sharp—knives, razor blades, needles, and so forth.)

I remember reading Pushkin's poem "I Remember a Wondrous Moment." When I was in the Red Army during World War II, I met a nurse, Natasha. She was so young and so beautiful, but there was no time for falling in love. A few days later I became a prisoner. To my great surprise, a group of Russian prisoners were brought to our camp—and among them was the unforgettable Natasha. But only three days later I was transferred to another prison. Only God knows what happened to her. But I remember Pushkin's poem, and Natasha.

I remember, in the beginning of the war, hearing again and again from our guards: "I am happy to be a German, I am happy to be a German soldier."

I remember a piece of real bread that the prisoners received in honor of Hitler's birthday, the twentieth of April. I don't remember the birthdays of my parents.

I remember how a physician, a fellow prisoner, pulled my two wisdom teeth while we were in prison. I had awful pain and the doctor told me, "Since you speak German, go to them and ask them for some alcohol and a pair of pliers. When you have done this, find two strong men among the prisoners." I found everything, and the operation was performed.

I remember reading Hitler's *Mein Kampf* in the original and feeling the weight of its declaration that only Aryans are human beings; other races are to be exterminated or enslaved.

I remember a time in prison camp. A guard called me, urging me to help him understand what one prisoner was trying to tell him.

The prisoner was a Russian Mennonite who could not speak German. Despite imprisonment, the spirit of the Mennonite remained intact. I was very much impressed with that spirit. He was trying to tell the guard that he was freer than the guard, because it was only his body that was imprisoned and not his soul. He urged the guard to understand that, as a guard, he was chained to the rifle. The rifle was chained to the army, and the army was chained to the ideology of Hitler. But Christ taught to love and, if necessary, to die in service, not to enhance the power of a dictator.

When I translated all this to the guard, he became furious. Here a prisoner was trying to teach a guard, a superior! He called the prisoner a dirty pig.

"It doesn't matter what I am," the Mennonite replied. "I still love you. The time might come when you realize your own mistakes."

The guard warned him, "You had better disappear from my sight, or I'll kill you."

But the Mennonite again replied, "You can kill my body but you will never kill my spirit. No matter what you say or do, I still love you."

At that time I couldn't fully understand the message of the Mennonite, but I could feel the force of it. It became of great value to me later in my thinking, living, and teaching. I now wonder what happened to that guard and that Mennonite.

I remember visiting the battlefield of Verdun in France. It was one of the most devastating battle sights of World War I.

There is a bell tower there. Each day at sunset the bell rings to remind the living of the ever so many thousands that died there. Underneath the tower there is an enormous room filled with human bones of unknown soldiers—one of the grimmest monuments to war. Around the tower there are cemeteries: American, Belgian, German, British, French. There are over twenty thousand crosses in the American cemetery alone.

There is a grave just outside the French cemetery with no cross. The guide told us, "This is a pacifist who refused to go and kill others. Therefore he is not admitted to the company of the others." Those who killed the most received iron crosses. Those average soldiers who died received wooden crosses. Those who refused to kill received no cross, the symbol of Christ, whose message was to love and serve. Isn't that the irony of human existence?

I remember how much the Russian prisoners exhibited their skill under awful conditions: some wrote poetry, some played musical instruments, some carved wooden toys. All this kept their spirits alive. Creativity is one of the highest forms of happiness, especially in prisons.

I remember a German guard asking a Russian prisoner, "Why do you sing here so often?" The Russian replied, "The brave sing in prison. The cowards sing in churches or when ordered."

I remember seeing the first V-1s and V-2s, the previews to coming attractions.

I remember various jobs: loading and unloading the railroad cars, digging trenches, slaving in stone quarries. But worst of all were the jobs of cleaning and restoring the bombed out towns and cities: dust, dirt, awful smell, and the angry guards. I remember specifically living through an inferno named Berlin in 1944. Men, women, and children anguished in the rubble of once-upon-a-time streets. People had been swept away by molten asphalt during the burning crescendo of an American air raid. It is now that the guards would say: *"Ich hab' den Krieg nicht gewollt"* (I did not want this war).

I remember the anarchic madness of the final battle. I was north of Berlin at that time, flanked on both sides by evernearing fronts. When it became clear to the Germans that their situation was hopeless, our guards dropped their posts and fled. We who desperately didn't want to be caught in a Soviet-British exchange fled to the south—to Munich and then to Salzburg.

I remember, during the last days of World War II, hearing on the radio that Hitler had died in the battle of Berlin. About ten or fifteen minutes later we heard a shot. An S.S. man had committed suicide. With no *führer,* there was no direction or meaning to his life.

A "Displaced Person"

I remember when I became free after 1,313 days in German captivity. I decided to go to one farmer and ask if I could work for him and stay for a while. He agreed. I needed time to settle down and to see what would happen. Those who decided to go back to Russia were met with a cruel reception. The best that could happen to them would be to go to Siberia. There were instances where the British and the Americans forced the Russians to go back to Russia because of the Yalta agreement. It was a tragic moment in history.

I remember going from that farm to Salzburg, Austria. After one week I found a job in Mozart's Festival House working as a stagehand. One of my interesting jobs was to help create an impression of a waterfall. We stuck feathers into rollers, and from a distance one would really believe it was falling water.

I remember the Rosittenkaserne—army barracks in Salzburg—being renovated into a camp for displaced persons. I lived there for four years after the war before I departed for America—a German-speaking Russian, completely unversed in English.

I remember once in the Festival House I shouted something to a worker. The director of the plays heard and asked, "Why don't you come with me? I want to place you upon Moenchsberg to see whether I can hear your voice shouting *'Jedermann!'* like a voice from heaven." So I did. I was in the rehearsal of the play shouting that word.

I remember the days I learned to climb mountains while living in Salzburg. On top of a mountain like Untersberg, staying overnight in an alpine hut and waking up very early in the morning with the sun about to rise, one is in the land of fairy tales. Hundreds of mountaintops covered with ice and snow suddenly see light. Gradually it spreads over the mountaintops. It is truly a breathtaking sight. Nowadays you can get there by cable car.

I remember visiting my friend in the hospital in Oberndorf, about twenty miles from Salzburg. The friend had tuberculosis, and, as the railroads had not been repaired from the war yet, I had to walk. While I was staying there, my friend asked me to remain overnight and go to church that evening.

In the evening I went to church. It was filled with people. In front there was a boys' choir. Then the announcement came: "This is the annual performance of 'Stille Nacht, Heilige Nacht,' which we've performed here from the very beginning of its creation." I still thank my friend for having me stay.

I remember how, after losing my job in Mozart's Festival House, I was employed by the American army unit, first as a dishwasher and later as a second cook.

I remember the morning I made pancakes for American soldiers. The mess sergeant was sick, the first cook drunk, and I, the civilian second cook, spoke no English. Three cantankerous gasoline stoves and 140 hungry men made quite a mess of the mess hall that morning.

I remember how the hungry Austrians at the end of World War II came to American army kitchens to get whatever food they could out of the garbage cans.

I remember when President Truman and the Congress of the United States passed a bill to admit 205,000 refugees to this country. I became one of them.

I remember Mr. and Mrs. Dahlen, who were living in Salzburg working with the Civil Intelligence Corps and who introduced me to Joseph Mow. It is through them that I was able to come to America. Joseph Mow, the Church of the Brethren representative to the Salzburg International Resettlement Office, helped me come to America. Joe is the son of Anna Mow, the modern saint of the Church of the Brethren.

I remember the series of medical examinations that qualified prospective U.S. immigrants. Those with tuberculosis had to remain in Europe. T.B. or not T.B.—that was the question.

I remember the USS *A.W. Greely* that took me and twelve hundred other displaced persons from Naples to New York. There is a saying: See Naples and die. I saw Naples and I wanted to see more.

I remember gigantic, light green, foamy-topped tornado waves in the Mediterranean. Sometimes I think of the terrors St. Paul must have gone through in the primitive crafts of his time. By contrast, I remember the mirror-smooth waters of the Atlantic by the Azores.

A New World

I remember seeing the Statue of Liberty from our ship as it entered the harbor of New York, as so many others have seen it. Years later I visited Staten Island and read the inscription. The author surely had tasted suffering herself.

I remember the brotherly care of those in Brethren Volunteer Service who brought several of us to New Windsor, Maryland, from New York. There at the Brethren Service Center, I spent my first night in America.

I remember my first days at Juniata College in Huntingdon, Pennsylvania, where I was offered a place to live, to work, and to study—American style.

I remember one of my first assignments at Juniata: to sheet some fifty beds in the men's gym. Several students from the dormitory where I lived, hearing of my plight, volunteered to help me. We completed the chore painlessly. I carried the blankets and sheets and they made the beds. I was happy that the job was done so cooperatively. I basked in the warmth of the camaraderie until the first guests arrived. First one, and then a bantering volley of voices, demanded who had made these beds. They had all been short-sheeted. Emerson's essay on self-reliance still comes to my mind.

I remember a friendly visit by two senior students, Howard Long and Peter Meyer, who came to my room my first day at Juniata. Peter, an Austrian student, served as an interpreter. Each time I see Howard now, it reminds me of that visit.

I remember a couple of veterans who came to my room the same evening and invited me for a glass of beer on 13th Street. The veterans of the fifties changed the social life at Juniata. They were more aggressive and didn't pay attention to the strict traditions on campus. Dancing was introduced, and dances were held in the women's gym, a building that has since been demolished.

I remember my first meal on the campus when Miss Mathias, the director of food service, asked me what I would like to drink. I said, "A glass of beer."

Everyone at the table seemed paralyzed. My neighbor on the left, Harold Brumbaugh, assistant to the president, informed me, "We don't drink here." The atmosphere at the table slowly returned to normal.

I remember how my neighbor told me the next morning that the people of Huntingdon were saying a Russian spy had arrived.

I remember meeting President Calvert Ellis in his office. He welcomed me to the Juniata community and said that if I needed any help I shouldn't hesitate to come to his office. I felt the warmth and sincerity of this welcome and was impressed that the president of the college would take time for an insignificant man and be genuinely concerned with his affairs.

I remember my first boss, Mr. Guy Hall, the foreman overseeing a dozen janitors, some ground workers, and a carpenter. Nowadays I see three or four men with walkie-talkies riding on a cart.

I remember how the janitors, telling jokes during the lunch period, used words that I couldn't find in the dictionary. When I became a student, I discovered there is a dictionary of slang and unconventional English to help one in such situations.

I remember being accused of not shouting loudly enough, "Man on the hall!" when I had to pick up garbage from the women's dormitory. I shouted as loudly as I could, I think.

I remember Charles Rowland, professor of music at Juniata College. As a janitor in Swigart Hall, once in a while (while cleaning the piano keys) I would hum some song. One time Professor Rowland came to me and said, "George, I think you have a very good voice. Let's see if you can sing." At first I was bashful and wouldn't do it, but he persisted and eventually I gave in. After I'd sung for a while, Professor Rowland stopped and said, "Well, George, I played the white keys and I played the black keys, but you sang in the cracks." And that ended my music lessons with Professor Rowland.

I remember Dr. Fayette McKenzie, professor emeritus of sociology, who taught me English while I was working as a janitor on the campus. Each weekday after work, I went to his home in Taylor Highlands. We started by reading the Bible in basic English. I remember his remarks: "We proclaim Jesus Christ as our Lord and Saviour without following him. We are hypocrites." I thought it took courage to say that.

I remember Ken and Jane Crosby who invited me to their home for dinner. Since that time it is not only their home, but also their hearts that are open to me. It was through their encouragement that I went to college to study. Ken became my first professor in America.

I remember the first course I took at Juniata during the summer of 1950. It was American history taught by Ken Crosby. When I teach Russian, I always think of that course and how hard it was for me to be completely immersed in the process of learning a foreign language. It has made me sensitive toward my students.

I remember when I became a student I attended chapel, where many speakers began their talks by stating, "The world is shrinking." I recall the words of the student next to me: "It's not the world that's shrinking—it's your head!"

I remember a young sociology professor, a graduate of the University of Chicago (regarded then as a progressive university), who challenged his students with the statement, "There is no god. If there is one, prove it." One of the students dared to say, "If there is no

God, prove it." Whether one was right and the other wrong, that is not the issue. The professor's contract was not renewed.

I remember how complicated American college life seemed to me. There were so many opportunities to choose from that I never seemed to have any free time for myself.

In Russia university life was much simpler. First of all, all educational classes began at the same time each year, whether in the first grade or at a university. They all began on September first. There were no electives; everyone took the prescribed set of courses for his or her specific field.

In my experience at Juniata, however, there were all sorts of extracurricular activities: Mountain Day, Homecoming, Parent's Day, chapel choir, chapel convocation, theatrical and musical productions, clubs of all sorts, peace fellowship, band and orchestra, sports clubs, May Day, freshman initiation, dormitory rivalry, roommates' pranks, honor society, touring choir, ministerium, formal dances, etc., etc. How simple my life in Russia and Europe was! How many things in the United States one has to consider either to enter or avoid.

I remember a seminar on national security in the fall of 1950. It was held in Washington, D.C., and organized by the Quakers. With several other students, I made my first trip to Washington and had a chance to observe the American government in operation. We visited the House of Representatives and also had a chance to talk to our Senators. I was already using the word *our,* although I was not yet a citizen of the United States.

During this time I discovered how difficult it was to find a place to eat in Washington. We had a couple of black students with us, and they were not admitted to the restaurants. I felt very strange about this. As a foreigner, I had an advantage over blacks who were natives of the country. I felt ashamed that I was admitted and they were not. Blacks prepared the food, they served the food, but they could not eat it together with the whites. We had to leave the city to find a place to eat together.

With these experiences during the seminar, the main idea of the Quakers began to take hold of my mind and soul: the oneness of human nature. The message of George Fox—that there is a part of God within everyone—became very important to me. I began to pursue a study of Quaker history.

I remember John Biddle, the late publisher of the Huntingdon *Daily News,* and his lecture on Rudyard Kipling. He started the lecture with a joke: Two ladies were talking. One asked the other, "Do you like Kipling?" The other lady replied, "Honestly, dear, I don't know how to kipple." It was the first joke that I understood in English, and I was proud of myself.

I remember Dr. Edgar Kiracofe, professor of education at Juniata, who introduced me to the history of education as well as to two prominent American philosophers—William James and John Dewey. I clearly remember that James and Dewey rejected any form of cosmic determinism, religious or scientific. They emphasized a radically empirical philosophy that they called pragmatism—that is, change is the only constant. They also asserted that truth is relative, experience is determinative, and consequences supply meaning.

In Dewey, this philosophy became instrumentalism: truth as an instrument for reforming and remaking the world. He also stressed James's discussion of the goddess success in American reality and the affliction of stress that accompanied her, with all her demands for sacrifice.

James said that all is in flux—the universe emerging, evolving, growing, decaying—not even God knows how it will come out. To me, this pronouncement was revolutionary—what one calls a real American philosophy.

I remember beginning to visit the Stone Church of the Brethren soon after I arrived in Huntingdon. I was very much impressed with the friendliness of the people, with their warmth—and especially with the sermons by John Middlekauff, whose main messages were pacifism, service, and reconciliation. After spending so many years in the army and in prison, it was a joy to find people in America who said openly that they would not fight and that it is better to live in peace and follow the commandments of Christ. This appealed to me more than any other new idea I discovered in this country. I decided to continue visiting the Stone Church until it became quite natural for me to worship there.

I remember my first feetwashing service at the Stone Church in Huntingdon. I was sitting next to Ken Crosby. When the service was over, I realized how meaningful the experience had been for me. At that time I was a janitor, and a professor had washed my feet. Suddenly I felt that there was no distinction. We were all human, with all the qualities that come with being human. This ceremony remains one of the most meaningful for me in the Church of the Brethren. I recall reading that the Russian Orthodox Church has feetwashing, but it is only for the bishops, not for the ordinary people.

I remember how John Middlekauff, pastor of the Stone Church, and Dr. Tobias Henry (who was a deacon of the church at the time) came to my room and invited me to become a member of the church. I was very much surprised by this as I thought I already was a member. When I told them I had been baptized by trine immersion in the Russian Orthodox Church, they felt it was no problem for me to join the Church of the Brethren, which also practiced trine immersion. I am a member to this day and am very happy with the Stone Church.

I remember my first basketball game, back when Juniata played downtown in the high school. A group of students took me. Just before the game, I saw a group of girls come out onto the floor. I asked someone, "Who are they?"

"These are the cheerleaders," he told me. "Aren't they cute?"

"Yes," I agreed, "but what are they going to do, play basketball?"

"No. they will cheer our team to victory."

It reminded me of the *Tacitus Germania*, where the battles between the Romans and the Teutons are described. Wives of the Teutons were in the background spanking their children, urging the fathers to victory. I suspect they were the first cheerleaders. But the Teutons defeated the Romans. Juniata lost that game.

I remember an annual All Class Night in 1951 in which I played the role of a music critic. On stage, President Truman asked me a question: "What do you think of my daughter's musical ability?" I was instructed by the director to say, "She stinks." President Truman then pulled out a gun and killed me. I was horrified. How could one do this publicly, on stage before an audience—talk about the president of the country and the members of his family? But this is America. In Russia, and perhaps other countries, this would have been unthinkable.

I remember when I was accepted as a graduate student at the University of Pennsylvania in the Department of Germanic Languages and Literatures. I was interviewed by a Dr. Springer, the head of the department, and I was offered a teaching assistantship. Through Dr. Springer I became acquainted with the wealth of the German medieval epics, primarily with *Tristan and Isolde, Parsifal,* the *Song of the Nibelungs,* and others. In order to really study the medieval epic, one must first study Middle High German. This then is the key that opens the field. It's so beautiful and impressive that a person must really do it himself or herself in order to be able to fully appreciate the work.

I remember Dr. Ernst Jockers, a doctor of literature, with whom I worked as a graduate student at the University of Pennsylvania. He taught major German authors. He loved Goethe so much that he dressed like Goethe, he spoke like Goethe, he wrote like Goethe—he knew everything about Goethe. Fred Pohorille, George Avery, and I would go to a 7:00 to 9:00 evening seminar at his home. Very seldom did we leave his house before 11:00, and very often it was midnight. Yet sometimes at midnight he would serve sandwiches and beer and continue talking until 2:00 or 3:00 in the morning. How often can one find a professor so dedicated, having so much knowledge of his field, and loving to teach?

I remember German honorary fraternity meetings, again with Dr. Jockers. It was hard to believe how he could inspire us to drink, to sing, to crawl under tables, naturally, all in German.

I remember Dr. Vladmir Sajkovic, chairman of the Russian department at the University of Pennsylvania. Through him and his wife Miriam, I was introduced to the wealth and depth of Dostoyevsky.

I remember meeting Barbara McClure, a graduate of Juniata, while I was a student at the University of Pennsylvania. She was working at the university as a librarian. I spent delightful hours with her at the Academy of Music listening to great performers. The most unforgettable performance was that of Igor Stravinsky conducting his own works. When he conducted *Petrushka,* I was completely mesmerized. I was in another world, forgetting reality while enjoying immersion in his world of art.

I remember the summer I found a job in Ocean City, New Jersey, through the university's placement office. It was a place called Simms' Seafood Restaurant.

When Mr. Simms asked me if I could cook, I told him that I could cook some. He said that they needed a sandwich maker. I asked, "What kind of sandwiches am I expected to make?"

He told me, "We only have seventy-five kinds."

"I'll need a year to learn!" I said. But he put me to work right away. I was always impressed by American on-the-job training. And sure enough, little by little I learned to make seventy-five different kinds of sandwiches.

I liked the job. The hours were regular, it paid well, and I had Mondays off. These Mondays a group of us would go deep-sea fishing. There were so many fish I'd get tired of pulling them in. My first catch was a baby shark. The excitement on the boat was so great that when I pulled it out, one of the fishermen pulled out a knife and killed it—not even asking me about it. I thought perhaps it was custom.

I worked in that restaurant for two summers. The second summer United Press International learned that I was to return to Juniata as a professor. A journalist and cameraman came, asked me several questions, and took a few pictures. The next day my picture—with about forty dinner plates in my arms—appeared in most newspapers in the United States. People would come and ask, "Who's George? Where's that Russian?" Suddenly I was a celebrity. The waitresses got so tired of it that they just put a sign in front of my sandwich stand that said, "I am George." I still have that sign.

Later I talked to Juniata College President Binder about my experiences in Simms' Restaurant, and he told me that the restaurant no longer exists. A video arcade stands in its place. It is sad, but things change. Yet I learned not only how to make sandwiches there, but how to work with others, how to serve others, and how to enjoy life.

I remember living on 240 South 39th Street, a noisy area. A fellow graduate of Juniata Joe Thomasburger (at that time a graduate student at Crozier Seminary in Chester) suggested that I move to Chester. They needed someone who would teach students German so that they could pass their doctoral examination.

It was one of the best moves of my life. The scenery was beautiful, the setting was peaceful. I received a room, vacated (I was told) by Martin Luther King, Jr., who had graduated. It was the perfect place to do graduate work. I had my books, I had peace, I had inspiration from both people and nature.

I had to commute from Chester to the University of Pennsylvania. I remember a big sign as one comes into Chester: "What Chester makes makes Chester." I guess one can apply this slogan to anyone. What one does, makes one.

I remember being asked, upon returning to Juniata as a member of the faculty, to live as a proctor with the students in a dormitory called Cloister. I was responsible for order and discipline. I had a good relationship with the students. However, there were a few incidents.

One day I returned from my lecture to find my door had disappeared. I had a bell I would ring to assemble students, so I rang it. When they came I asked, "What happened to my door?" They grinned and said nothing. I told them, "I will give you thirty minutes to bring my door back." I left and came back thirty minutes later to find my door in place.

One of the students asked, "What would you have done if we hadn't brought the door back?" I told him I didn't know. But my door remained in place after that.

Naturally there were problems with noise in the dormitory, sometimes in the middle of the night. After two years I felt I'd had enough, but how could I get out of it?

I remember a visit to the cliffs with a girl who told me the Alfarata legend:

"Many, many years ago, before civilization had penetrated into the heart of these mountains, the Indians held this country as the happy hunting-ground of the earth: Black Cloud, their chieftain, was admired by all the tribes for his great strength and boldness. But even a greater admiration was held for his winsome Indian daughter, Alfarata. Her spirit was as brave as that of her father's, her body as lithe as that of a deer, her eyes sparkled like diamonds when the noonday sun shone upon them, and her cheeks bore the blush of the early dawn. Alfarata spent much time dreaming of the purity of the stream that flowed by her Indian lodge, of the greatness of the mountains, of the azure of the sky, and her heart was filled with the lure of romance.

"One day, as was her custom, she struck out in her canoe and glided down the waters of the Blue Juniata. On and on she went until she realized that, by the position of the sun in the skies, it was time for her to return. Just as she was turning her canoe, she noticed the figure of a stranger on the bank. He was paler than anyone she had ever seen, but her heart thrilled at the thought of his beauty. Nearer to the shore the maiden drew and listened to the strange, thrilling story of this white adventurer. Departing,

Alfarata reluctantly promised to return the next day, lured by the novelty of the experience and thrilled with romantic adventure.

"Many dawns broke, and every day, just as the sun was travelling toward the west, Alfarata and the stranger met. Beneath the shades of the great trees where the waters murmured softly, the stranger whispered words of love to the Indian maid. Unconsciously the heart of the maid answered the call of the man just as naturally as the deer seeks the wholesome wild. Often the white man had urged Alfarata to leave her primitive home and go with him but she hesitated because of her father's command that she marry one of her own tribe.

"But as autumn drew near and the leaves turned to red and gold, the two hearts answered the call of love. One morning, before the sun had dimmed the stars, Alfarata carefully stole forth from the lodge to the secret call of her lover. She paddled noiselessly down the river and met the expectant one. All day long they turned bends of streams and glided on and on through peaceful valleys, and together they dreamed of the golden hours that awaited them. When the stars gleamed in the sky, they stopped and near the shore built a campfire which was to be the only hearth they would ever know.

"As they sat dreaming of all their joys, suddenly a war cry sounded in the air. Instantly Alfarata knew that Black Cloud had followed and had discovered them. But nothing could daunt the young lovers. The bride clung to her young protector and as swiftly as the arrow sped through the air, so swiftly did the souls of these two escape. The dying embers of the campfire alone were left; for the Goddess of Love had come to their aid. But always the spirit of these two lovers shall gleam in the stars of love and passion and shall ever guide those whom love calls through life's changing cloud and sunshine" (*Alfarata*, Juniata College Yearbook, 1922).

After hearing this story I began dreaming of my Alfarata.

A New Home

I remember beginning to consider marriage and starting to "shop around" a little bit. I told someone and the news spread very quickly across the campus.

The dean of women, Mrs. Dove, approached me and said, "George, I don't think there is any girl for you here on the campus. They are either too young like the students or too old like myself." I figured she was an experienced lady, so I assured her I would "shop" someplace else.

That night I went to visit my friends Bob and Gala Higinbotham, who lived in Alexandria, just seven miles from Huntingdon. Gala was born in Siberia in 1922. When the revolution occurred, her family left Russia and went to China. From China they went to Japan, and during World War II Bob Higinbotham, as an officer, met Gala. They fell in love, got married, and settled in Alexandria. I established a good friendship with them.

While I was there that evening, Gala told me a neighbor would be stopping by. The neighbor was Billie Lang who told me that she had a single sister, Joanne Phillips. I told Billie that I would certainly like to meet a single woman.

So the next weekend Joanne came from Philadelphia where she worked at the Museum of Natural History as a backdrop painter. We hit it off immediately.

In Germany there is a song *"Ich hab' mein Herz in Heidelberg verloren."* But my song is "I lost my heart in Alexandria." I dated Joanne for almost a year. We were engaged and married. Two years later we had a son, Gregory.

Very often I think one of the best solutions for world problems is intermarriages of people from different countries and different cultures. When I see a White marry a Black, when I see a German marry an American, when I see a Russian marry a German, it makes me very happy. I know that they have to work harder, but it is with this hard work that one learns so much about the differences. Joanne and I have been married thirty-seven years and our marriage is very strong. We are happy.

I remember seeing our son in the maternity ward for the first time. I experienced the strange feeling that I would be called "father" from then on. What had I done to deserve this title, this name "father"? I felt almost ashamed, for I hadn't done much. It was my wife, his mother, who carried him, nurtured him, and brought him to life.

I remember when I came to Juniata there was an experimental atomic station in Saxton. The station was visited by Swiss engineers. I was asked to go and help them out.

I went to Saxton and met the management of the station and the Swiss engineers. We decided to have several meetings so I could explain the vocabulary. The next day I was scheduled to come in the evening. So I asked the manager of the station how I could get past the gate. "Just come in your car," he said, "open the window, and shout 'Westinghouse!'"

So I did. I came, shouted "Westinghouse," the gate opened, and I entered. I went to the office with all the drawings and information, and I thought, Isn't that strange? I just came from Russia, and yet everything is open to me. Trustful Americans.

I remember talking to students in middle and high schools of Huntingdon County. Each time I spoke, there were literally hundreds of questions. The younger they were, the more questions they asked. I cannot help thinking how ignorant the Americans are of Russian realities and how ignorant the Russians are of American realities. There is such a great need for all nations of the world to open their borders and, most of all, to open their hearts and souls in order to learn about each other's needs.

I remember being very happy with my career of teaching German at Juniata. I introduced scientific German, the German major, and Middle High German literature. Then in 1957 the Russians launched Sputnik into space, and President Ellis asked me to teach Russian at Juniata. I agreed. I thought I would like to teach my native language, but I had no graduate experience in Russian.

President Ellis suggested I apply for a scholarship. I followed his advice, applying for a Danforth Foundation scholarship for teachers. I filled out the applications, had a personal interview, and received the fellowship: first to go to Middlebury College and then to Harvard to study Slavic languages and literatures. For three years (including two summers) I studied at Harvard. It is there that I became thoroughly acquainted with the history, literature, and language of Russia and other Slavic nations.

Upon fulfilling the residency requirements for a Ph.D., I returned to Juniata to teach Russian. I had very good students, some of whom now teach; some are in the navy chasing Russian submarines.

I remember learning so much about the great writers—especially Pushkin, Gogol, Turgenev, Dostoyevsky, Tolstoy, and Chekhov—while at Harvard. I am especially grateful to Professor Roman Yacobson, a great linguist, for introducing me to Russian medieval literature. With all these experiences I returned to Juniata. I offered Russian, first one course, then two, three; then Russian area studies; independent studies; and individual instruction in Russian.

I remember the Widener Library at Harvard, where I read and learned so much about the American idealists: Channing, Garrison, Emerson, Thoreau, and their influence on Tolstoy.

I remember the Russian Orthodox-Brethren exchange in 1963. The purposes were as follows: "To establish a bridge of understanding between a Christian church in America and a Christian church in Russia. To provide opportunity for the Church of the Brethren and the Orthodox Church of Russia to share informally concerns and viewpoints on reconciliation and international peace on the basis of Christian brotherhood and with a nonpolitical emphasis. To emphasize a people-to-people type program in contrast to an exchange of high level officials." I was to serve as the official interpreter for this program and very much enjoyed being in the position where I could help others arrive at an understanding.

I remember many of the things that impressed the Russian priests. They began to realize how strong American religious life is, not only on its own, but also as recognized by the government. When they first came, the Russians were allowed only twenty-five miles of free movement. But when the Church of the Brethren promised Washington that they would be responsible for the group, the State Department gave them permission to go anywhere.

The Russians were impressed by actions of the Church of the Brethren against war, as I had been when I arrived in the United States.

They discovered differences in our religious services, especially when it came to singing. In Russia only the choir sings, but here the entire congregation sings.

They were inspired by the vesper service at the lake at Camp Alexander Mack. There was preaching, singing, and a mutual feeling of peace. One of the priests said, "Wouldn't it be nice to live like we are here in this camp?"

The Russians were surprised that the Brethren knew each other, no matter where they were. One priest even asked me if it was prearranged to make them believe that the Brethren are so friendly to each other. But when I told him about the history of the Brethren, when I told him that often ten percent of the membership attends Annual Conference, he began to understand.

The Russians were impressed with Bethany Seminary and with the General Offices in Elgin. They were impressed with the friendliness and real concern for the well-being of the priests and the Russian Orthodox Church.

There was one interesting experience at Millersville College, Pennsylvania. The people there tried to impress the Russians with their technology. They showed off their electronics, and the Russians would just say, "Oh, we have that." But on the way back from the physics lab, one priest spotted something on the wall and asked what it was. I told him it was a pencil sharpener. The priest called the other priests over to look at it. I pulled out a pencil and sharpened it. We spent thirty minutes looking at and talking about the pencil sharpener! Before they left the country, every priest received, in addition to all kinds of other presents, a pencil sharpener.

Throughout the encounter many asked, "Are you Communists? Are you spies? Are you trying to undermine our security here? Or are you really Christians?"

The best answer I can recall was given by one priest: "In 1935 my church was destroyed and I was sent to Siberia. After fourteen years of hard labor, I returned to rebuild my church. I am in charge of it now. What do you think?" Answers like that were very helpful to Americans in understanding what it means to be a member of the Orthodox Church in Russia. Americans take freedom, civil or religious, for granted. The Russians have to fight for them.

After the exchange was over, while flying home, I wrote the following lines:

A Russian priest

        while touring the United States

was asked

       after his after-dinner speech:

"How do you like America

      and how do you find our food?"

Pondering for a moment,

     the priest began

         with a quiver in his voice:

"I lived through nine hundred days,

          each day a year,

in the besieged city of Leningrad.

     Eight hundred thousand died

of sheer starvation.

     In order to survive

we ate tree roots, cats, dogs, and rats …

     And now,

beholding the richness and variety of sustenance

     upon this table,

what can I say?

     And still, I must confess

I am hungry for a bowl of borsch

     and a piece of real Russian rye bread."

In our times experiences such as these should be supported. It is through efforts like these that people can bring themselves to understanding, working through the conflicts.

I remember finding a piece of paper on the sidewalk on my way home from class. I picked it up. It was a letter from a girl to a boy. It said at the end, "Dave, I love you. I love you now and I will love you forever."

I am often challenged by certain phrases. And one of them is "forever." What does that mean?

I read the same thing in a Windham College catalogue concerning the solicitation of funds for scholarships, fellowships, assistantships, and so forth. The form said, "I bequeath (a certain amount of money) to establish (a fund) to perpetuate the name of (someone) forever." Windham College doesn't exist anymore. What does forever mean?

When I was in Washington for the first time, I went to the Lincoln Memorial. Above Lincoln's head on the back wall, I read the words, "In this temple, as in the hearts of those for whom he saved the union, the memory of Abraham Lincoln is enshrined forever."

Then there is the Lord's Prayer: "For thine is the kingdom and the power and the glory forever." What is forever?

I remember my 1965 experience of teaching Russian at Indiana University in Bloomington. I had ten students who were so good that no matter what I gave them to learn, they would ask me for more. Because they were so good, they inspired me even to write poetry in Russian. Some of them still write to me. I believe that more Americans should study Russian so that it will help them become better acquainted with the Russians and their culture.

I remember teaching Russian at Windham College during the summers of 1968 and 1969. It was a very progressive college, with almost no structure. For example, there were no grades given and there were no real subjects. Everything was done through inspiration, through personal relationships between faculty and students. It was a great idea. But every great idea needs certain form. I learned just recently that Windham College is closed. It lacked the structure that could keep the content viable for the benefit of the institution.

I remember the day when Joanne and I were appointed to a position of directors of the Brethren Colleges Abroad Program in Marburg, Germany.

We traveled on a German boat, the *Bremen*, in July 1970. The night before we were to arrive in Germany, I could not sleep. The past was so alive in me again. A German boat, a German servant, the German language… There I was, returning to a country where I'd spent so many days in prison.

And suddenly I thought of the sergeant. I remembered his name and that he came from Frankfurt. I began thinking, I'll settle in Marburg. Then I'll go to Frankfurt and do everything possible to find the sergeant. What if I find him? What will I do? I will go to a place where I can make my shoes muddy, I will throw them in front of him and say, "There. Clean them and polish them." What if he refuses? I will buy a pistol. If he refuses, I'll kill him.

With all these thoughts in my head, I couldn't sleep all night. In the morning, when we got up, Joanne asked, "Why are you so pale? You look so tired."

I told her I didn't know.

Then I opened the door and there were my shoes. The servant had polished them, without my even asking. I was so amazed. A German had polished my shoes! I thanked God.

Suddenly I smiled. The burden of all the memories that had accumulated during the night had been relieved. Joanne saw my smile and asked what had happened. I told her that it was a beautiful day.

Now when I polish shoes at home and people compliment us, Joanne says, "Oh, George likes to do that." People ask me if that's true and I say, "Yes, especially for those whom I love."

I remember my Swiss trip with Joanne and Gregory. We were in Lucerne. It was not far from a village called Altdorf. When I was a small boy I read William Tell's story: how the father had to shoot an apple off the head of his son with a bow and arrow. We decided to take a train to see where, according to legend, that event took place.

It was a beautiful train ride. When we arrived, we were given the history. It was in Lucerne that someone suggested we take the cable to the top of a mountain so that we could see the entire area. Two or three days later, Gregory went with me up Mt. Pilatus. It was the most beautiful view of the Alps. Many of the mountaintops were covered with ice, and the sun shining on them looked like thousands of candles burning. Around us we could see the lake covered with fog. Gregory—who is now grown—still says this is one of the most unforgettable experiences of his life.

I remember when Joanne and I met M. R. Zigler at Hedda and Don Durnbaugh's apartment in Marburg. I can still hear him saying, "I wish the Christian churches would advance in their spiritual maturity instead of moving in circles, repeating the same mistakes." For over fifty years he worked for the cause of peace. It is men like M. R. who deserve the Nobel Peace Prize.

I remember our flight from London to New York. We were sitting in the middle of the plane. Suddenly we saw a pilot coming. He knelt right at the feet of my wife and was looking around as if to discover something. Joanne asked him gently, "Is anything wrong?"

He answered, also gently, "The landing gear froze."

Right away my imagination flew. Now we would be in an awful state at landing. But I was so much impressed with the pilot's composure. He lifted the carpet, tested the temperature, and then told us quietly, "We have to descend, we're flying too high. I'm sure everything will be all right." He assured us, he assured himself, and he went back to the cockpit. Several hours later we had a smooth landing. But these are the moments one doesn't forget!

I remember returning from Germany to Huntingdon and finding that there had been a flood. Our basement was filled with water. When everything had been cleaned up, everyone said, "Wasn't it nice how people cooperated?"

The flood united so many people in helping each other, in compassion and consideration. Why can't we learn to be cooperative when there is no flood, when there is no threat of disaster? It will be too late to be united if something as horrible as an atomic war comes along.

I remember speaking at a father-son banquet about the German roots of the Church of the Brethren. When I finished my speech by reciting the Lord's Prayer in German, an old man came to me with tears in his eyes. He told me that I brought back wonderful memories. His father had taught him the Lord's Prayer in German, but he hadn't recited it later in life. After seventy years, the entire memory of his childhood returned. I was so happy to do this for him by simply reciting a prayer.

I remember spending a long weekend at Pendle Hill, a Quaker center for study and contemplation. I lived in one room. It is a beautiful place where a person can have a peaceful and meaningful spiritual life if one really wants to discover that part of God that is within.

On my desk in the room, there was a notice about meeting for worship. It said: "This meeting is sometimes called worship on the basis of silence, sometimes on the basis of listening, or worship through contemplation, or simply meditation. For some it is a turning inward as for a beginning or continuing of an inward journey. For some it is a meeting with God or waiting upon God. There need be no embarrassment or discomfort if the entire period remains silent. While speaking is often evidence of the vitality of the meeting, there is a living silence of even greater power. Meeting is always an adventure for Quakers or anyone who would like to discover the spiritual values within himself."

I remember introducing a unit at Juniata called "Friends and Brothers, Studies in Historic Peace Churches: Brethren, Mennonite, Quaker." As I wrote in the objectives: "This unit will offer theoretical learning and field study opportunities. It will deal primarily with history, beliefs, practices of the historic peace churches with an emphasis on pietism, pacifism, nonconformism and other distinctive characteristics. To give this study a more specific character, the history of Juniata College will be scrutinized in light of her Brethren heritage."

I also remember inviting Reuben Hess from the Old German Baptist Brethren Church to join Kim Hill, a member of my class, in a discussion of the past, present, and future of the two churches. The Brethren and the Old German Baptist Brethren Church were one before 1881. Is it possible that both will become one again? The publication of *The Brethren Encyclopedia* may be a step in that direction.

I remember a seminar on "Building a Sustainable Society," held at American University. Lester Brown, who heads the Worldwatch Institute, said, "We have not inherited the earth from our fathers. We are borrowing it from our children."

Through history we've always had prophets who were so sensitive that they cried to the multitudes to change their ways of life. I regard Lester Brown as one modern prophet. Naturally there are many more. I think the time is here to listen to the prophets so that they do not cry in the wilderness.

I remember reading in a book by Michael Binyon, *Life in Russia,* "Most Russians simply cannot imagine that they could ever be in the wrong; that their country could ever do something unacceptable to the rest of the world." I've lived in many countries and I can say the same thing about the Germans, the French, the Italians, the Americans, and so on. We have to be more critical of ourselves. We can be critical when we get together and learn about each other and, most of all, about ourselves.

I remember, as a member of the Peace and Conflict Studies Committee of Juniata College, I was asked to submit a number of quotations by various people on war and peace. These quotations, along with other related material, appeared later in a booth that was placed by our committee in the hall where the National Democratic Convention took place in San Francisco in July of 1984. The following quotations were chosen by the committee:

"An eye for an eye will make the world blind."

—Gandhi (1869-1948)

"There never was a good war or a bad peace."

—Benjamin Franklin (1709-1790), American statesman

"War and peace were the rhythm of history, like night and day. Can we have peace without war?"

—Lance Morrow (*Time*, May 17, 1982)

"Where apathy is the master, all men are slaves."

—an old proverb

"Since wars begin in the minds of men, it is in the minds of men that the defenses of peace must be constructed."

—United Nations Declaration

"Yes, 130 million Americans might be dead, and another 32 million might be injured. But the remaining 61 million healthy survivors can rebuild the country and live long, productive lives if they use common sense and follow government guidelines."

—Ed Zuckerman (*Esquire*, March 1982)

Senator Proxmire:

"What do you think is the prospect, then, of nuclear war?"

Admiral Rickover:

"I think we will probably destroy ourselves."

I think the time has come to realize that the Americans and the Russians have a mutual enemy: atomic war. Fear is an irrational force that can lead to mutual destruction. Fear comes not from God, but from the devil. In order to turn fear into trust, we have to turn away from the devil toward God. And the devil is not just someplace, it is within us. It appears that there are people who want to propagate fear. Let us listen to those who propagate love and to the best voices in our own hearts.

I remember meeting the Russian poet Yevgeny Yevtushenko for the first time at Harvard University in 1960 when he read his poetry there. About sixty students and members of the faculty were waiting in the classroom for him to appear. From the moment he appeared to the moment when he left the room, he gave the impression that he was born to be a poet, to be an actor performing his own poetry. He read many of his poems, all of them known by heart, and he talked about his life. He said his autobiography was his poetry. One poem he read, "Babii Yar," was dedicated to the tens of thousands of Jews executed by the Nazis at the Babii Yar ravine near Kiev in 1941 and brought him some forty thousand letters from his readers. Dmitry Shostakovich set this poem to music.

While staying at Harvard, Yevtushenko wrote a poem that he named "The American Nightingale." I recall its last six lines:

> All nightingales understand each other.
> They speak one language everywhere.
> Their singing is delicate and tender.
> They are united in their art.
> But what about us people,
> How long shall we remain strangers to each other?

I remember the time when Joanne and I attended the Chautauqua Conference on United States-Soviet Relations, from June 22 to June 29, 1985. The week's program included presentations by scientists, diplomats, artists, and entertainers from the Soviet Union and the United States. The morning lectures, afternoon seminars, and evening performances covered a wide range of topics from nuclear arms reduction and human rights to poetry and jazz. One memorable experience was an evening program when Yevgeny Yevtushenko joined the American jazz saxophonist Paul Winter and the Paul

Winter consort in "A Concert for the Earth," a mixture of songs and poetry about the environment and about animals. The event was a celebration of nature, the common heritage of all nations.

The Yevtushenko-Winter partnership began with a performance in front of the United Nations General Assembly. After that, they successfully toured the United States and the Soviet Union together. The *New York Times* called these joint efforts a prototype for the healing human dialogue between these two countries.

Two years later, with the strong support of President Robert Neff, Yevtushenko came to Juniata College. Oller Hall was full; there was standing room only.

He read and he talked and he touched on many themes, especially on nature, art, love, war, death, and the suffering of people around the world. The audience was not disappointed. He and his friend received a standing ovation.

Years later, at the Juniata College commencement on Sunday, May 12, 1991, an honorary doctorate in humane letters was presented to Yevtushenko. He started his address to the graduating class with the question, "Why is it that so many young people commit suicide?" He continued, "Do not be afraid when you suffer. Remember that total pessimism is no less stupid than total optimism. Remember that the rainbow of life has a full spectrum, including the darkest colors. You should accept suffering willingly, but you should be fearful if you suffer only for yourself and not for others." Long before he became a poet of *glasnost* and *perestroyka,* Yevtushenko warned in this poem about Stalin's heirs, published in a 1962 issue of the *Pravda* newspaper:

> We rooted him out of the Mausoleum,
> But how shall we root Stalin
> Out of Stalin's heirs?

It is Stalin's heirs who have become the challengers to Yeltsin's authority and who undermine his programs of democratization and private enterprise in Russia.

I remember the summer of 1974, when I offered an unusual course at Juniata College. Participants studied "Aspects of American and Russian Culture." They compared the two countries' political and economic structures and their contributions to the world's art and religion. As part of the course, I organized an icon exhibit on a budget of twenty-five dollars.

In 1987, I remembered that one thousand years ago (988 A.D.) Christianity was introduced to Old Kiev. According to the ancient chronicles, it was in that city that the Russian lands took birth. To celebrate that historic event, I gathered a committee to organize an expanded Russian icon exhibit. Bob Wagoner, who became a workhorse for the project, said: "If we want to have an excellent exhibit, we have to have appropriate icons together with brochures, posters, and a catalog." I liked his "we." Immediately I remembered the twenty-five dollars we worked with to produce the first exhibit.

On April 4, 1988, Juniata College announced the opening of the exhibit in Shoemaker Gallery: "Russian Icons of the Golden Age, 1400-1700." The icons of the exhibit came from the collections of Alex Latsinik of New York, Reverend Ledlie Laughlin of Greenwich Village, and Dr. Hugo Polak of Connecticut. In addition, thirty-two icons, the bulk of the display, came from the collection of Koitcho and Tatiana Beltchev, who live in Switzerland. The Fogg Art Museum of Harvard University also contributed two icons. Dr. Natalia Teteriatnikov, curator at Dumbarton Oaks in Washington, and her husband, Vladimir, a scholar and art restorer, helped us with research and with preparation of the catalog.

The exhibit traveled to the National Cathedral in Washington, D.C., and enjoyed showings in New York City; Lafayette College in Easton, Pennsylvania; the College of the Holy Cross in Worcester, Massachusetts; and the Frick Art Museum in Pittsburgh. The exhibit was a great success.

I remember May 1988, when I retired after thirty-four years of teaching German and Russian. I received a telephone call from Mrs. Elizabeth Baker, whose main interests in life were theater and peace. She and her husband, John C. Baker, chairman emeritus of the Juniata Board of Trustees, started a "Peace and Conflict

Studies Program" at Juniata in 1971 and later at Bethany Theological Seminary and Ohio University.

"George, I heard that you've retired from your teaching. I remember one morning when John and I visited and enjoyed your class, 'Studies in the Historic Peace Churches: the Brethren, Mennonites, and Quakers.' " She went on: "Since you don't have much to do now, I thought of introducing you to a project that's very important for our times. Have you heard of a book called *Peace Pilgrim?*"

"Yes," I answered. "I not only have heard of it but I have the book, I've read it, and I like it."

"Splendid," she said. "I would like to suggest that you translate this book into Russian."

"That is an interesting idea, and I'll think about it," I said.

"Don't think. Start now."

Soon I received the texts and began to work. It was not only my knowledge of Russian that inspired me to do the translation. It was also Peace Pilgrim's complete devotion, dedication, and service to the cause of peace—peace among nations, peace among groups, peace among individuals, and that very important inner peace.

Of her countless messages, I would like to stress several here: Decide about your life's calling and follow it with dedication; once you make this decision, you will find you have boundless energy. Be willing to face life and life's problems squarely. While trying to solve any problem, look first of all for the causes of the problem. Always remember to observe the problem's symptoms. Simplify your life. Simple living brings great freedom. Keep your body clean; purify your thoughts and desires; and the spiritual life is the real life. All people can be peace workers. Peace Pilgrim's main message asserts, "This is the way of peace: Overcome evil with good, falsehood with truth, and hatred with love."

Jeff Blom of the Peace Pilgrim Center in California later told me, "Seventy thousand copies of your translation of Peace Pilgrim's book are about to be printed in Moscow for distribution in Russian, and another twelve thousand will be printed here.... Your great efforts are bearing much fruit."

I remember being asked whether I expected such drastic and fast-developing changes in the Soviet Union; my friends also wondered what had caused these changes. It was easy to answer the first question by saying that there were vague and uncertain predictions about the future of the Soviet empire, but the world at large was surprised by the events that changed not only the Soviet Union, but also the rest of the world.

As for what effected the changes, one can suggest a whole list, including these:

- The unstable life and turbulent developments in the Soviet Union throughout the twentieth century: World War I, 1913-1917; the February and October revolutions of 1917; the Civil War, 1918-1921, which claimed an estimated twenty million lives; Stalin, who came to power in 1929, forced industrialization and collectivization of agriculture, fought a war against religion, purged countless "enemies of the state" and, in this process, put to death an estimated twenty-three million Soviet people; World War II, 1941-1945, in which official statements indicate that the Soviet Union lost twenty million lives, but some researchers speak about twenty-seven million. Altogether, the country had a loss of some seventy million people, seventy million voices asking, What did we die for? Was all our suffering in vain?

- Ideological disagreements that led to a split between China and the Soviet Union. The situation became so serious that it caused Adrei Amalrik, in 1970, to write his book *Will the Soviet Union Survive Until 1984?*

- The period of "thaw" at Stalin's death in 1953, when Khrushchev began his de-Stalinizing work.

- The challenging and uncompromising efforts of many Soviet dissidents, especially Andrei Sakharov and Alexander Solzhenitsyn. In their open letters, petitions, manifestos, and publications at home and abroad, they stressed that the Soviet Union was in the midst of a terrible economic, political, ideological, and moral crisis.

- Tito's revolt against Stalin, the revolution in Hungary, the workers' riots in Poland and East Germany, and the organized protests in Czechoslovakia and other Soviet satellites, all of which undermined the stability of the communist world.

- Modem communication media, such as satellite radio and television broadcasts. These enlightened the Soviet people after the Communist Party had so long kept the public ignorant about many of the world events.

- The unsuccessful war in Afghanistan and the stagnation under Brezhnev and his successors, Chernenko and Andropov.

All this and much more left every Soviet citizen asking, *Shto dyelat*? (What should be done?). In response to this question, a youthful, dynamic, idealistic man came to power in 1985. His name was Mikhail Gorbachev. He, likened to Moses, Copernicus, Martin Luther, Darwin, Abraham Lincoln, F.D.R., Freud, Mussolini, General Franco, Don Quixote, and others, became a leader of a peaceful revolution with two themes: *glasnost* (openness) and *perestroyka* (restructuring).

In less than five years, he was able to accomplish the following: he eliminated medium-range missiles and ended the Cold War; replaced old-guard politicians with new, liberal-minded ones; withdrew Soviet troops from Afghanistan; granted more freedom and tolerance to churches and related institutions; ended the Communist Party's right to a power monopoly; allowed for the free election of a Russian president; endorsed the gradual move toward a market economy; and proclaimed that each nation had the right to rule itself without intervention from outside. Exercising that right, the German people tore down the Berlin Wall and the two Germanies reunited.

For all this, *Time* magazine named Gorbachev the "Man of the Decade," and he also received the Nobel Peace Prize. I think that by doing too much too fast for the hard-liners and by not doing enough or not doing it fast enough for the reformers, Gorbachev was caught in between, pressed from both sides. In the weeks that followed, he was not able to control the developments either in the party or in the country, or to provide sound leadership. Life became harder, goods became more scarce and more expensive—but worst of all, the Soviet Union was falling apart.

While Gorbachev was vacationing in the Crimea, the hard-liners under Gennady Yanayev staged a coup to reverse the course of developments in the country, but the heroic leader Boris Yeltsin, once Gorbachev's ally but now his rival, saw that the coup was threatening to lead the country back to a dictatorship. Yeltsin assumed leadership of the progressive forces in a revolution that ended the dictatorship of the Communist Party and its components. *Newsweek* proclaimed 1991 the "Year of Yeltsin." The poet Yevtushenko, along with Yeltsin and other revolutionaries, hailed August 19, 1991, as a historic moment that would long be remembered.

It is important to know who will head the government in Moscow, but the most important lesson the Russian people still have to learn is how to govern themselves democratically on both the local and the national levels. An active democracy is the best way to keep the society free from oppressive totalitarian rulers. Democracy will inspire material and artistic creativity and ensure stability not only in Russia, but also in other parts of the world.

I remember one of my students asking me, "What is your greatest wish?" I replied, "My greatest wish is to see Americans and Russians joined by other peoples of the world in living and working together, enjoying the fruits of their labor, in playing and singing, rejoicing in celebration of the greatest gift from God: the gift of life."